FOR

Heather

FROM:

Joni Nation

DATE:

12-25-14

Compiled by Kathy Shutt.

ISBN 978-1-61626-626-4

Published by Barbour Publishing, Inc., P.O. Box 719, Uhrichsville, Ohio 44683, www.barbourbooks.com

Our mission is to publish and distribute inspirational products offering exceptional value and biblical encouragement to the masses.

Member of the
Evangelical Christian
Publishers Association

Printed in China.

"MOM" -ISMS

Wit, Wisdom, and Humor for a Mother's Heart

BARBOUR
PUBLISHING

You can fool all of the people some of the time,
and some of the people all of the time,
but you can't fool Mom.

Captain Penny

When your mother asks,

"Do you want a piece of advice?"

it is a mere formality. It doesn't matter if you answer

yes or no. You're going to get it anyway.

Erma Bombeck

There is only one pretty child in the world,
and every mother has it.

Chinese Proverb

Mother is the name for God on the lips and
in the hearts of little children.

WILLIAM MAKEPEACE THACKERAY

Only mothers can think of the future—
because they give birth to it in their children.

Maxim Gorky

A mother's arms are made of tenderness,
and children sleep soundly in them.

VICTOR HUGO

Working mothers are guinea pigs in a scientific experiment to show that sleep is not necessary to human life.

UNKNOWN

Mother love is the fuel that enables a normal human being to do the impossible.

MARION C. GARRETTY

I love my mother, as the trees love water,
and sunshine—she helps me grow,
prosper,, and reach great heights.

ADABELLA RADICI

God could not be everywhere,

so He created mothers.

JEWISH PROVERB

In peace I will lie down and sleep,
for you alone, LORD, make me dwell in safety.

PSALM 4:8 NIV

A suburban mother's role is to deliver children obstetrically once, and by car forever after.

PETER DE VRIES

To a child, "home" is always where Mother is.

Youth fades; love droops;
the leaves of friendship fall;
A mother's secret hope outlives them all.

Oliver Wendell Holmes

Some mothers are kissing mothers and some are scolding mothers, but it is love just the same, and most mothers kiss and scold together.

PEARL S. BUCK

A mother's happiness is like a beacon,
lighting up the future but reflected also on the past
in the guise of fond memories.

HONORÉ DE BALZAC

It is said that children brighten a home—
they never turn off the lights.

UNKNOWN

No one in the world can take the place
of your mother. Right or wrong,
from her viewpoint you are always right.
She may scold you for little things,
but never for the big ones.

HARRY TRUMAN

You know you're a mother when you've said:
"Don't ask me; ask your father."

Making the decision to have a child is momentous.
It is to decide forever to have your heart go walking
around outside your body.

Elizabeth Stone

She is clothed with strength and dignity,
and she laughs without fear of the future.

PROVERBS 31:25 NLT

All mothers are working mothers.

UNKNOWN

There is no way to be a perfect mother,
and a million ways to be a good one.

JILL CHURCHILL

The precursor of the mirror is the mother's face.

D. W. Winnicott

My mother had a slender, small body,
but a large heart—a heart so large that
everybody's joys found welcome in it,
and hospitable accommodation.

Mark Twain

Mother—that was the bank where we deposited all our hurts and worries.

T. DeWitt Talmage

Mom Perspective: My teenage daughter thinks I'm too nosy. At least that's what she keeps writing in her diary.

Unknown

Every beetle is a gazelle in the eyes of its mother.

Moorish Proverb

All that I am or ever hope to be,

I owe to my angel Mother.

ABRAHAM LINCOLN

The phrase “working mother” is redundant.

Jane Sellman

Her children rise up and bless her;
her husband also, and he praises her, saying:
"Many daughters have done nobly,
but you excel them all."

PROVERBS 31:28–29 NASB

Mother's love is peace.
It need not be acquired,
it need not be deserved.

ERICH FROMM

When you are a mother,
you are never really alone in your thoughts.
A mother always has to think twice,
once for herself and once for her child.

Sophia Loren

Cleaning up with children around
is like shoveling during a blizzard.

Unknown

A mother is not a person to lean on,
but a person to make leaning unnecessary.

Dorothy Canfield

It's not easy being a mother.
If it were easy, fathers would do it.

UNKNOWN

Being a full-time mother is one of the highest salaried jobs. . .since the payment is pure love.

Mildred B. Vermont

Mommy Brain: When your gray matter turns into gray hair.

Ian Nelson

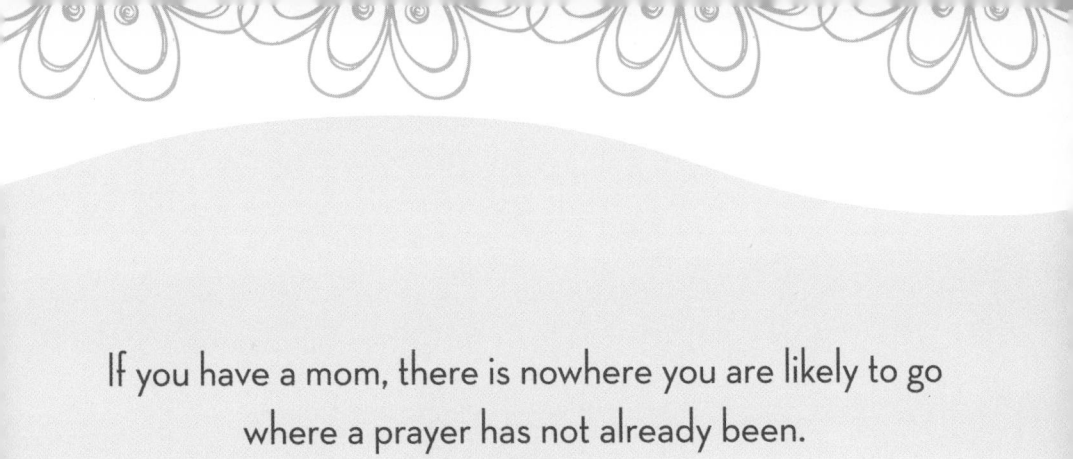

If you have a mom, there is nowhere you are likely to go
where a prayer has not already been.

Robert Brault

If there were no schools to take the children away
from home part of the time,
the insane asylum would be filled with mothers.

EDGAR WATSON HOWE

He renews my strength.
He guides me along right paths,
bringing honor to his name.

PSALM 23:3 NLT

Mothers hold their children's hands
for a short while, but their hearts forever.

Unknown

The moment a child is born,
the mother is also born.
She never existed before.
The woman existed,
but the mother, never.
A mother is something absolutely new.

RAJNEESH

Every time I close the door on reality,
it comes in through the windows.

JENNIFER YANE

A mother understands what
a child does not say.

UNKNOWN

I remember my mother's prayers
and they have always followed me.
They have clung to me all my life.

ABRAHAM LINCOLN

You don't really understand human nature unless you know
why a child on a merry-go-round will wave at his parents
every time around—and why his parents
will always wave back.

William D. Tammeus

You know you're a mother when you've said:
"Were you raised in a barn? Close the door!"

Definition from the *Dictionary of Mom.*

BECAUSE: A mom's reason for having her children do things that can't be explained logically.

Most mothers are instinctive philosophers.

HARRIET BEECHER STOWE

Direct your children onto the right path,
and when they are older, they will not leave it.

PROVERBS 22:6 NLT

Before a day was over,
Home comes the rover,
For mother's kiss—sweeter this
Than any other thing!

William Allingham

Where we love is home—home that our feet may leave, but not our hearts.

OLIVER WENDELL HOLMES

Things are going to get a lot worse
before they get worse.

LILY TOMLIN

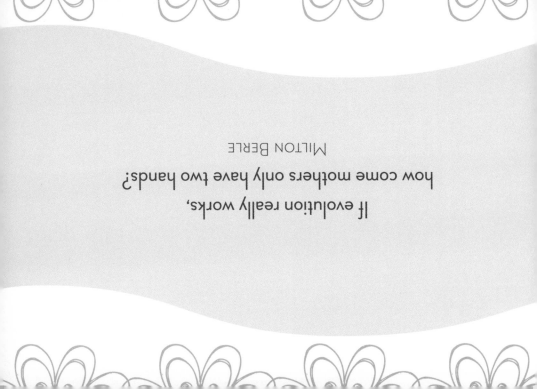

If evolution really works,
how come mothers only have two hands?

Milton Berle

A man's work is from sun to sun,
but a mother's work is never done.

UNKNOWN

The hand that rocks the cradle usually
is attached to someone who isn't
getting enough sleep.

JOHN FIEBIG

All women become like their mothers.
That is their tragedy.
No man does. That's his.

Oscar Wilde

You know you're a mother when you've said:
"Get your elbows off the table."

I try to take one day at a time,
but sometimes several days attack me at once.

Jennifer Yane

You should clothe yourselves instead
with the beauty that comes from within,
the unfading beauty of a gentle and quiet spirit,
which is so precious to God.

1 PETER 3:4 NLT

My mother's menu consisted of two choices:

take it or leave it.

Buddy Hackett

What my mother believed about cooking was that if you worked hard and prospered, someone else would do it for you.

NORA EPHRON

Of all the rights of women,
the greatest is to be a mother.

LIN YUTANG

The hardest job you'll ever love
is being a mother.

Unknown

Definition from the *Dictionary of Mom*.

I SAID SO: According to Mom, reason enough.

Who is it that loves me and will love me forever
with an affection which no chance, no misery,
no crime of mine can do away?—It is you, my mother.

THOMAS CARLYLE

When God thought of mother,
He must have laughed with satisfaction
and framed it quickly—so rich, so deep, so divine,
so full of soul, power, and beauty was the conception.

HENRY WARD BEECHER

I'd like to be the ideal mother,
but I'm too busy raising kids.

Unknown

I think my life began with waking up
and loving my mother's face.

George Eliot

No discipline seems pleasant at the time, but painful. Later on, however, it produces a harvest of righteousness and peace for those who have been trained by it.

Hebrews 12:11 NIV

You know you're a mother when you've said:
"Who said life was supposed to be fair?"

Most children threaten at times
to run away from home.
This is the only thing that
keeps some parents going.

PHYLLIS DILLER

Mothers reflect God's
loving presence on earth.

William R. Webb

There is no friendship, no love,
like that of the parent for the child.

HENRY WARD BEECHER

A mother is the truest friend we have, when trials,
heavy and sudden, fall upon us; when adversity takes the
place of prosperity; when friends who rejoice with us in our
sunshine, desert us when troubles thicken around us,
still will she cling to us, and endeavor by her kind precepts
and counsels to dissipate the clouds of darkness,
and cause peace to return to our hearts.

WASHINGTON IRVING

Mothers of teenagers know
why animals eat their young.

UNKNOWN

A mother's love for her child is like nothing else in the world. It knows no law, no pity, it dares all things and crushes down remorselessly all that stands in its path.

AGATHA CHRISTIE

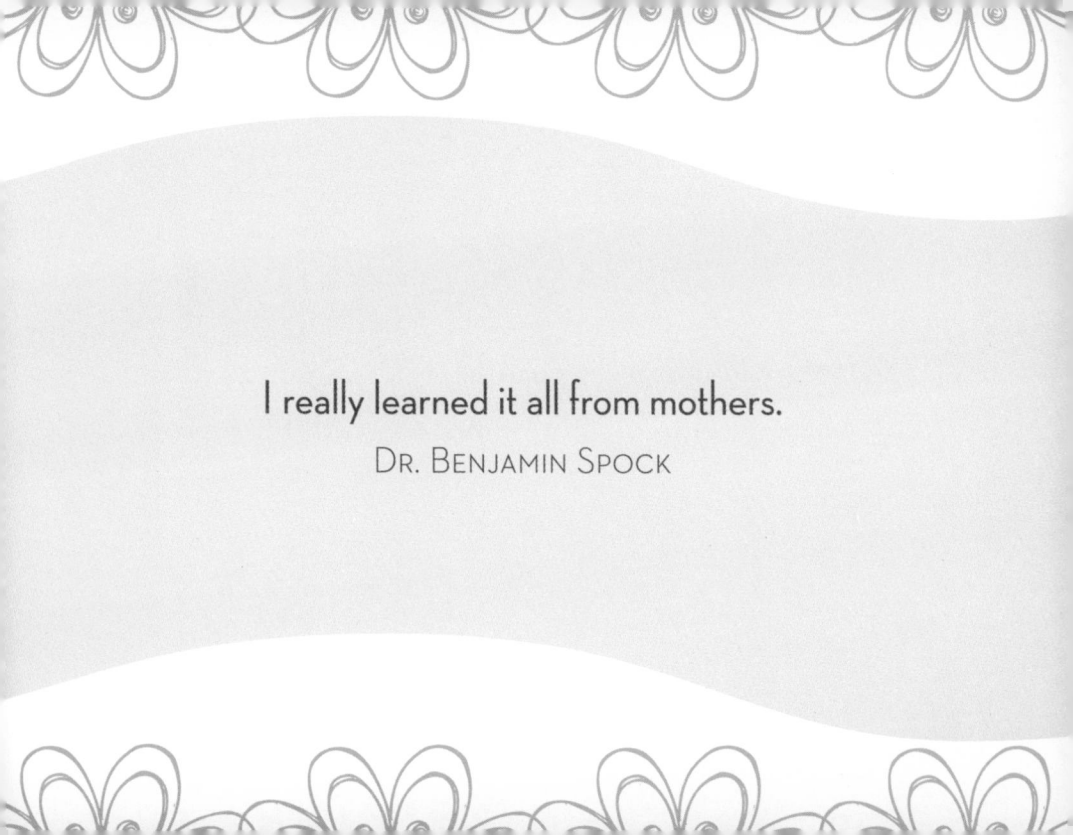

I really learned it all from mothers.

DR. BENJAMIN SPOCK

I want my children to have all the things I couldn't afford. Then I want to move in with them.

PHYLLIS DILLER

Charm is deceptive, and beauty does not last;
but a woman who fears the Lord will be greatly
praised. Reward her for all she has done.
Let her deeds publicly declare her praise.

Proverbs 31:30–31 NLT

The most remarkable thing about my mother is that for thirty years she served the family nothing but leftovers. The original meal has never been found.

CALVIN TRILLIN

The mother loves her child most divinely,
not when she surrounds him with comfort and anticipates
his wants, but when she resolutely holds him to the highest
standards and is content with nothing less than his best.

HAMILTON WRIGHT MABIE

Education commences at the mother's knee,
and every word spoken within hearsay of little children
tends toward the formation of character.

Hosea Ballou

Mothers all want their sons to grow up to be president, but they don't want them to become politicians in the process.

JOHN FITZGERALD KENNEDY

A boy's best friend is his mother.

JOSEPH STEFANO

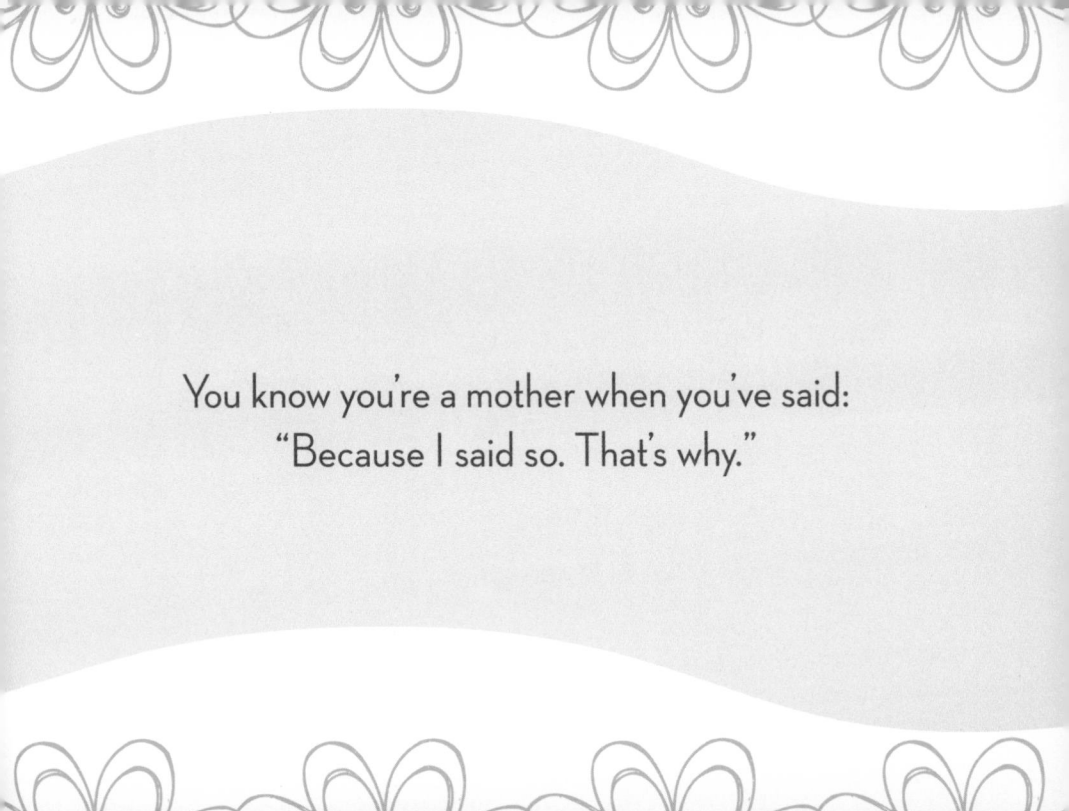

You know you're a mother when you've said:
"Because I said so. That's why."

Most of all the other beautiful things in life
come by twos and threes, by dozens and hundreds.
Plenty of roses, stars, sunsets, rainbows,
brothers and sisters, aunts and cousins,
but only one mother in the whole world.

KATE DOUGLAS WIGGIN

The worst feature of a new baby
is its mother's singing.

KIN HUBBARD

My mother had a great deal of trouble with me,
but I think she enjoyed it.

MARK TWAIN

When she speaks, her words are wise,
and she gives instructions with kindness.

PROVERBS 31:26 NLT

Motherhood is like Albania—you can't trust
the descriptions in the books, you have to go there.

Marni Jackson

You know you're a mother when you've said:

"If I didn't love you so much,
I wouldn't punish you. . . .
I would let you do whatever you wanted."

Definition from the *Dictionary of Mom.*

JOY RIDE: Going somewhere—sans kids.

To describe my mother would be to write about
a hurricane in its perfect power.

Maya Angelou

Over the years I have learned that motherhood
is much like an austere religious order,
the joining of which obligates one to relinquish
all claims to personal possessions.

NANCY STAHL

Men are what their mothers made them.

Ralph Waldo Emerson

A mother is a mother still,
The holiest thing alive.

SAMUEL TAYLOR COLERIDGE

Who, in their infinite wisdom,
decreed that Little League uniforms be white?
Certainly not a mother.

Erma Bombeck

Never say anything on the phone
that you wouldn't want your mother to hear. . . .

SYDNEY BIDDLE BARROWS

You are precious in My sight. . .

. . you are honored and I love you.

Isaiah 43:4 NASB

Children are a great comfort in your old age—
and they help you reach it faster, too.

Lionel Kauffman

The commonest fallacy among women is that simply having children makes one a mother—which is as absurd as believing that having a piano makes one a musician.

SYDNEY J. HARRIS

Children are the sum of what
mothers contribute to their lives.

UNKNOWN

I take my children everywhere,
but they always find their way back home.

ROBERT ORBEN

You know you're a mother when you've said:

"You're not leaving the house dressed like that!"

I've noticed that one thing about parents is that no matter what stage your child is in, the parents who have older children always tell you the next stage is worse.

DAVE BARRY

Before becoming a mother, I had a hundred theories on how to bring up children. Now I have seven children and only one theory: love them, especially when they least deserve to be loved.

KATE SAMPERI

Human beings are the only creatures
that allow their children to come back home.

Bill Cosby

I thought my mom's whole purpose
was to be my mom. That's how she made me feel.

NATASHA GREGSON WAGNER

May your father and mother rejoice;
may she who gave you birth be joyful!

PROVERBS 23:25 NIV

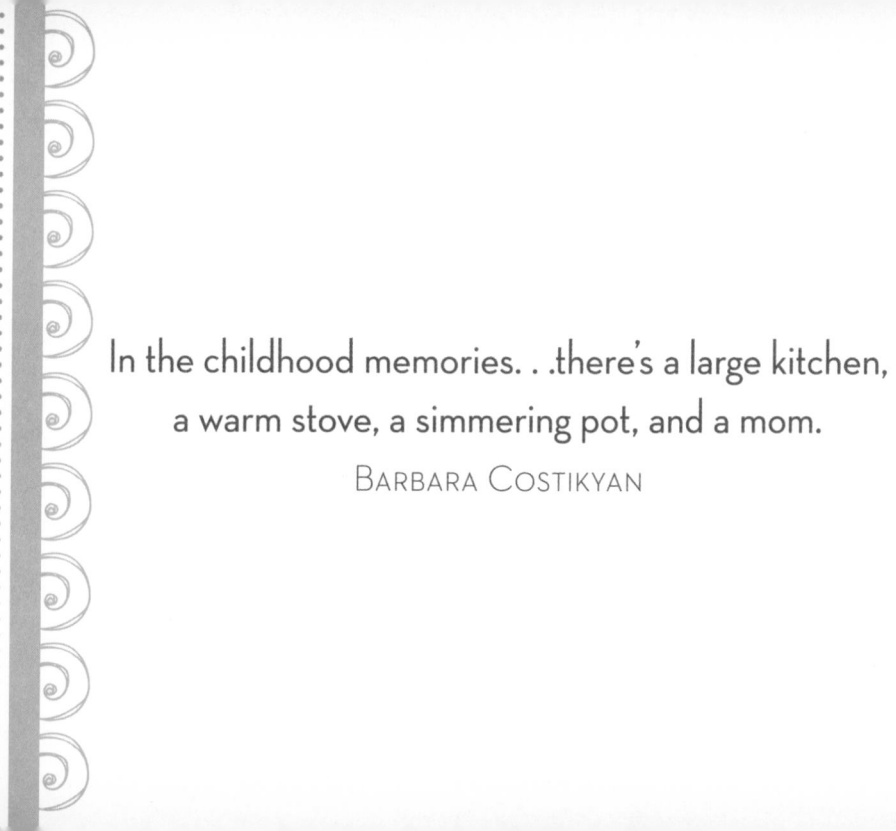

In the childhood memories. . .there's a large kitchen,
a warm stove, a simmering pot, and a mom.

Barbara Costikyan

Definition from the *Dictionary of Mom.*

YIPPEE!: Would be shouted by Mom if the school year gets changed to 12 months.

See also "YAHOO!"

Pretty much all the honest truth telling
there is in the world is done by children.

Oliver Wendell Holmes

"M" is for the million things she gave me,
"O" means only that she's growing old,
"T" is for the tears she shed to save me,
"H" is for her heart of purest gold;
"E" is for her eyes, with love-light shining,
"R" means right, and right she'll always be,
Put them all together, they spell "Mother,"
A word that means the world to me.

HOWARD JOHNSON

Mama exhorted her children at every opportunity to "jump at de sun." We might not land on the sun, but at least we would get off the ground.

Zora Neale Hurston

You know you're a mother when you've said:

"Don't use that tone with me!"

A man loves his sweetheart the most,
his wife the best, but his mother the longest.

Irish Proverb

Anyone who doesn’t miss the past never had a mother.

Gregory Nunn

No matter how old a mother is,
she watches her middle-aged children
for signs of improvement.

FLORIDA SCOTT-MAXWELL

The wise woman builds her house,
but the foolish tears it down
with her own hands.

PROVERBS 14:1 NASB

The hand that rocks the cradle
is the hand that rules the world.

WILLIAM ROSS WALLACE

There are only two things a child will share willingly: communicable diseases and its mother's age.

DR. BENJAMIN SPOCK

An ounce of mother is worth a pound of clergy.

SPANISH PROVERB

That best academy, a mother's knee.

James Russell Lowell

Motherhood is priced of God,
a price no man may dare
to lessen or misunderstand.

HELEN HUNT JACKSON

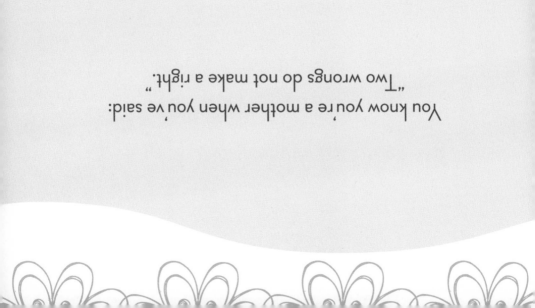

You know you're a mother when you've said:
"Two wrongs do not make a right."

Hundreds of dewdrops to greet the dawn,
Hundreds of bees in the purple clover,
Hundreds of butterflies on the lawn,
But only one mother the wide world over.

George Cooper

A father may turn his back on his child, brothers and sisters may become inveterate enemies, husbands may desert their wives, wives their husbands. But a mother's love endures through all.

WASHINGTON IRVING

She never quite leaves her children at home,
even when she doesn't take them along.

MARGARET CULKIN BANNING

[Love is not] rude.
It does not demand its own way.
It is not irritable, and it keeps no record of being wronged.

1 CORINTHIANS 13:5 NLT

A mom forgives us all our faults,
not to mention one or two we don't even have.

Robert Brault

Definition from the *Dictionary of Mom.*

KISS: Medicine applied by Mom.

Mothers are the necessity of invention.

BILL WATTERSON

With what price we pay for the glory of motherhood.

ISADORA DUNCAN

There's nothing like a mama-hug.

TERRI GUILLEMETS

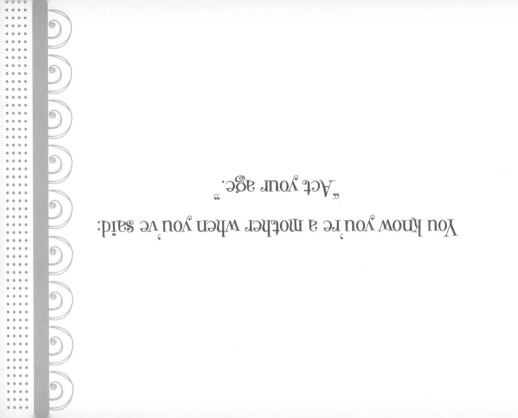

You know you're a mother when you've said:

"Act your age."

A mother is a person who seeing there are
only four pieces of pie for five people,
promptly announces she never did care for pie.

TENNEVA JORDAN

The best way to keep children home is to make the home atmosphere pleasant—and let the air out of the tires.

DOROTHY PARKER

By and large, mothers and housewives are the only workers who do not have regular time off. They are the great vacationless class.

ANNE MORROW LINDBERGH

Children are a gift from the LORD;
they are a reward from him.

PSALM 127:3 NLT

Mother's love grows by giving.

Charles Lamb

There never was a child so lovely,
but his mother was glad to get him asleep.

RALPH WALDO EMERSON

The tie which links mother and child is of such pure and immaculate strength as to be never violated.

WASHINGTON IRVING

Any mother could perform the jobs
of several air traffic controllers with ease.

LISA ALTHER

Ask your child what he wants
for dinner only if he's buying.

FRAN LEBOWITZ

It is amazing how quickly the kids learn the
operation of the DVD,
yet are unable to understand the vacuum cleaner.

ETIENNE MARCHAL

Each generation has been an education for us in different ways. The first child-with-bloody-nose was rushed to the emergency room. The fifth child-with-bloody-nose was told to go to the yard immediately and stop bleeding on the carpet.

ART LINKLETTER

A three-year-old child is a being who gets almost as much fun out of a fifty-six-dollar set of swings as it does out of finding a small green worm.

Bill Vaughan

The trouble with children is that
they are not returnable.

QUENTIN CRISP

The LORD is my shepherd; I have all that I need.

PSALM 23:1 NLT

You know you're a mother when you've said:

"Wipe your feet."

Raising a kid is part joy and
part guerilla warfare.

ED ASNER

Definition from the *Dictionary of Mom.*

MAYBE: No—most definitely no!

My mom is literally a part of me.
You can't say that about many people except relatives—
and organ donors.

Carrie Latet